Christma

Ten Poems to Give and Receive

ex libris

Candlestick Press

Published by:
Candlestick Press,
Diversity House, 72 Nottingham Road, Arnold, Nottingham UK NG5 6LF
www.candlestickpress.co.uk

Design and typesetting by Craig Twigg

Printed by Ratcliff & Roper Print Group, Nottinghamshire, UK

Cover illustration © Sarah Young, 2020
www.sarahyoung.co.uk

Candlestick Press monogram © Barbara Shaw, 2008

ISBN 978 907598 95 1

Acknowledgements

Thanks are due to all the copyright holders cited below for their kind permission:

Andre Bagoo, poem as yet unpublished, by kind permission of the author.

Suzannah V Evans, poem as yet unpublished, by kind permission of the author.

Mark Fiddes, poem as yet unpublished, by kind permission of the author.

John Greening, poem as yet unpublished, by kind permission of the author

Helen Ivory, poem as yet unpublished, by kind permission of the author.

John McCullough, poem as yet unpublished, by kind permission of the author.

Jessica Mookherjee, poem as yet unpublished, by kind permission of the author.

Pey Oh, poem as yet unpublished, by kind permission of the author.

Kelley Swain, poem as yet unpublished, by kind permission of the author.

Ben Wilkinson, poem as yet unpublished, by kind permission of the author.

Contents

This Year

If we could gift each other moments
I'd wrap up that bauble sun we felt
warm our backs to the tip of Mam Tor.

I'd box the two hours spent tracing
the tinselled reservoir, no two miles
the same as we ran and ran, trails

deserted, no sound but our own
good hearts and honest footfall. I'd
ribbon that first jog up Ringinglow,

our city held as if the snow globe
we'd shake. And I'd nestle under
the tree those loops of a floodlit track,

a reminder that what's done is done,
and of dark-bright moments still to come.

Ben Wilkinson

How to Grow Your Own Mistletoe

It's not possible to raise mistletoe
on any tree; rowan, lime and apple
are among the better hosts.

Harvest berries in the darkest spring
when absence threatens to fell the heart –
let this making-ready be a balm.

Now garner seeds and lodge them
in a tree's fostering hollow –
hessian will deny the prying beaks.

Let moon and earth do their rounds
while boy, then girl emerge lonesome
from their weatherhouse, never set to meet.

Mistletoe needs patience, but rest assured
the fact of it will live green on your threshold
and kisses will festoon you by and by.

Helen Ivory

Midwinter Gods

When light slows to a pinprick glow of sun and the bitter dark smirks
with a mouth that licks the ground with its silver tongue,
we three are still kids in the home of those gods, who in turn
are simply lost children too, abandoned in the noise of fading life.

I hear you ask me, what god will come this time? You say, school friends
in your class know his name, evoke him with brandy and sweet cakes,
open sacks so he can pour love in. I cup your face in my small hands
but can only tell you what I know, that our gods are carried by birds

and live inside leaves, clouds and dew. I go downstairs where the big god
reads his papers, checks stocks and shares. I ask him if this year
we can bring a tree inside. He sniffs, says *money's short, your mother's ill
and we are aliens in this land, our gods are not so generous.*

I steal twenty pounds from mother's purse and trip up the hill
to the local shops to buy glitter, pens, sweets and colouring books,
wrap them in bright paper, go into the night garden, pick berries, sharp
leaves and weeds that curl around my arms. I sing you to sleep

with tales of a god of gifts, who sleeps while leaves unfurl and wakes
when the world grows cold to warm you up with love. I make
our sister play the spoons outside your room and tell you
they're his sleigh bells on his way, watch you quite beside yourself

with eyes so wide at all my lies. We fill your pillow case with glittered jewels
and illuminated texts. In the morning you wake to find a room
covered with frosted leaves, berries and fairy lights. The god of gifts
has given you bright paper-wrapped mysteries. We stay with you,

stroke your hair, laugh at our godlike powers. Later we watch Morcambe
and Wise, fantasy films and play with all your toys. You ask me if our gods
still live in the wings of birds, I nod, they do and in the frost and the cupboard
under the stairs, but mainly they're in our hands. They do their best work there.

Jessica Mookherjee

For You, in the Winter Dark

I wish I could give you this gift of space.
Today, I can walk through green fields for an hour,
seeing no one. I can watch a skylark take flight from its nest,
watch red admirals bluster about in the wind.

I wish I could give you the fat smiling dandelions. And this gift of breath:
how the breeze, coming from the south, seems to flow through me,
loosening this corset of worry until I sigh easily again.

See? There is a hare, racing across the corn-rows, reminding us
of the meaning of distance.

I wish I could give you her leap, her caper, her absolute embodied freedom.

Kelley Swain

The Gifts

I remember the Christmas we went to the beach,
      the waves sweeping up rumours with broken glass.
I remember the Christmas we painted the accent wall, its pattern
      jagged, asymmetrical, a garden of forked paths.
I remember the Christmas I heard *parang* for the first time, a
      Spanish voice on the radio crying across the gulf.
I remember the Christmas we found a white tree in Excellent City
      and I wondered privately whether it was politically
      correct to have a white tree in a country without snow.
I remember the Christmas the poinsettia died.
I remember the Christmas we rang out the false and rang in
      the true.
I remember the Christmas I sat on the cold floor of the room
      I shared with my sister and held my new truck. It was red,
      white and blue, and I could tell Daddy was not happy,
      I could tell he did not love you. And still
I remember the Christmas when everything he touched turned to
      cigarette ash.
I remember the Christmas we dismantled the tree, putting its
      poems back into boxes, because the next day we had to
      move.
I remember the Christmas I looked at the candle and someone
      came and kissed me, no footsteps, no voice, lips unseen.
I remember the Christmas that was not really Christmas, but
      Carnival. People were liming in houses, going to fetes,
      dancing to soca, and each body was its own ornament.
I remember the Christmas I baked cookies and watched
      It's a Wonderful Life and there were hints of murder
      in James Stewart's eyes.
I remember the Christmas I looked at our tree, on which every
      finger had its ring, and felt there was no tomorrow
      but then the doors in the house opened into other
      scenes—some recounted, some foretold—and the
      gifts were waiting.

Andre Bagoo

The Gift of the Lotus/Liánhuā
Penang Island

At the equator, night falls as suddenly
as a plane can land. The whirr of the wing flap

shifts its tone, as my father's boyhood
reels past on the runway, new lights and factories

in a fluorescent glare where rice fields used to be,
and the roadside food stall

he liked to stop at
for fish congee after a long flight.

December may seem an empty month for her,
who radiantly came across the ferry from Mainland

as his bride one Christmas day.
Now there is no moon to chart the tide

that ebbs and flows around her feet.
A grief that never leaves her –

as ghosts of the past always seem to,
though they wash up abandoned

on beaches, silver
in the thick, hot dark.

Alone too, I can only offer kinship,
marzipan, M&S fruitcake, faint carols,

mixed spice of winter, holly-wreathed.
A foreign daughter come home

who must remind herself to unfold as a quiet lotus,
silent character of my father's mother's name.

Touchdown into this deep silt, hold on for dear life,
into the muck of it. When the monsoon thunders

overhead, *zen circle zen circle* is a whisper
round-leaved to myself. A perfect brushstroke

lightning-fast, gathering
enough strength

to lift my face up waiting –
for the balm of rain.

Pey Oh

You shouldn't have

Gold…Frankincense…Myrrh.
Bless. You shouldn't have.
Stick them over there.
Behind the I LOVE GALILEE sleepsuits.
Come a long way?
Landlord. Find somewhere for that lamb.
No, not the oven.
It's done something on the Lacroix napkins.
Who let the locals in anyway?
So cute. A carpentry set!
Always trust The Sanhedrin to get it right.
Don't show Joseph, He's always losing stuff.
They say it's his age.
Of course, we were both certain it was a girl.
Hence the pink fizz.
If you don't like champagne
I'm sure there's something stronger. Salome!
Be an angel.
Gorgeous!
Louboutin booties and an Audi baby stroller.
Will we ever find room in the workshop?
Get out of here!
A Platinum Card…Member since 00. Funny.
How did you guess his name?
Yes, I know it sounds like a footballer.
Not my choice, darling.
They're not the kind of family you mess with.
Let me guess.
You must be Cherubim and you Seraphim.
Nice jackets. I'm afraid the choir stays outside.
We're almost out of patisserie.
Where's my boy? Nobody puts baby in a corner.

Mark Fiddes

All I Want

'Music is a fair and glorious gift'
Martin Luther

Didn't you hear it, as you hunted for
a certain present, beyond *I wish
it could be* and *So here it is* –
the Salvation Army's muted *O
Holy Night*, or that little student
choir ascending close to *Gloria*
out on the fading high street?

I always heard it, even upstairs
wrapping something (you may say)
unsatisfactory for my parents:
a sound of war concealed within
Edwardian songsheets, my mother's
fingers to the boar's head voice
my father made: *If you haven't got
a ha'penny a farthing will do...*
                              And now,
at our very door? *In Dulci Jubilo?
Lullay, lullay?*
                  No, they were old,
those singers, even then, who used to call,
and no one teaches the tunes any more.
It will be just another delivery
of plastic swaddling. Scrooge's ruler
smashes at the letterbox, and a small
child runs away into
the darkness.
              So, put on King's
or summon Sir Malcolm Sargent: *Welcome,
Yule. There'll be a new world
beginning from tonight.*
                        Alexa, for Christmas
give me nothing but the sound of carols.

John Greening

Christmas at the Yard
After Francis Ponge

Winter, in the end, can be summed up by those white boats,
quiet swans covered with a thin layer of snow.

The boatbuilders work with bowed heads, shifting round the yard
like bright pieces of sunlight, puffing clouds into the sky.

Paperwork is done with mittened hands.

Nature unveils her bareboned self, brittle and branched,
silhouetted in late afternoon light.

She blows cool air into the workshop, hardens paint in tins,
strokes the yard cat with icy fingers until it mewls.

A cormorant dives and emerges in a tree ring of ripples,
a necklace of eels in its mouth.

In the powerhouse, presents are opened with gloved hands.
Faces are shining Christmas baubles.

Nature closes her eyes and dreams snow into the yard, where it falls, quietly,
until even the lemon yellow hull of the boat by the pontoon is obscured.

Suzannah V Evans

The Present

Christmas was pouring into neighbours' houses.
It was puddling on shelves, seeping out of cupboards

somewhere else. Meanwhile, our cat Flo's ears were burning.
Meanwhile, she wouldn't eat and shook and shook.

We raced by taxi to a vet, left her wailing.
The nurse next day said a urine test meant leukaemia

despite her vaccinations. *Her mother must've given it to her*
before she was born. All that time it had skulked

in her cells. Though I don't believe in prayer, I prayed.
We tacked up fairy lights, yanked them down.

No one expected the call, a second test coming back
negative. Her body was forming antibodies, still had a virus

but leukaemia? No. We took her home that day
and a week later she suddenly chased her sister round the tree.

Christmas, by that point, had grown fed up with waiting.
It battered down the door and flooded in.

John McCullough